Mel Bay Presents Stefan Grossman's Guitar Workshop Audio Series

Beginner's Fingerpicking Guitar

Ragtime, Pop, Blues and Jazz

taught by Fred Sokolow

For complete CD track listings, please see page 48.

1 2 3 4 5 6 7 8 9 0

Visit us on the Web at www.melbay.com — E-mail us at email@melbay.com

LESSON ONE
FOLK/POP FINGERPICKING
CHORDS

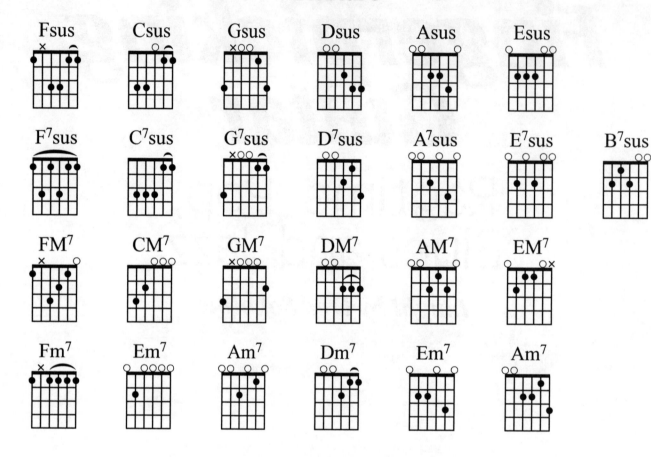

THE CIRCLE OF FIFTHS

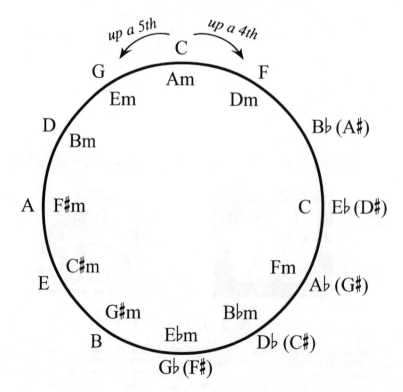

vi-ii-V-I PROGRESSION/KEY OF C

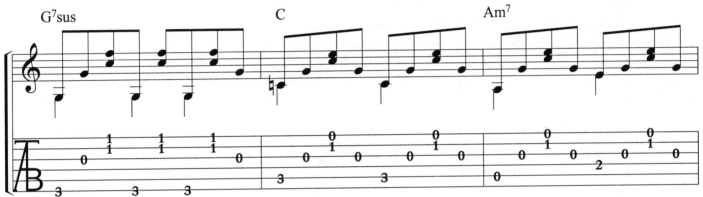

Note: lower case Roman numeral indicates minor chord, e.g. vi= VIm

vi-ii-V-I PROGRESSION/KEY OF G

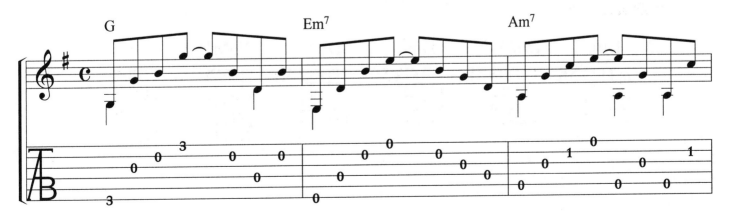

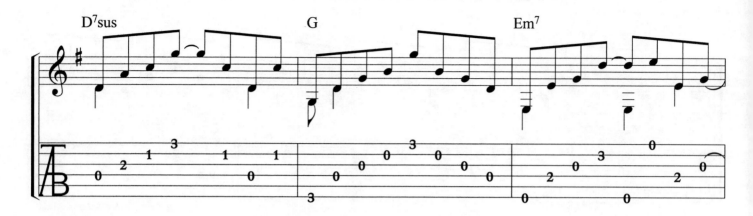

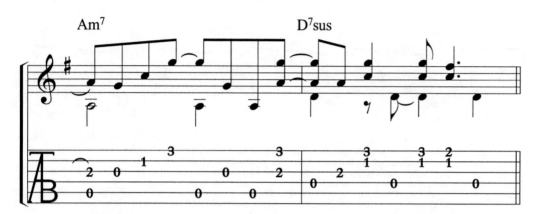

MINOR PROGRESSIONS, DESCENDING BASS

in A minor

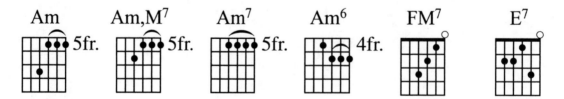

in D minor

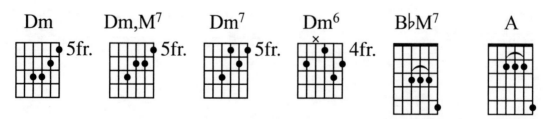

RHYTHM — STRAIGHT 4/4 FEEL

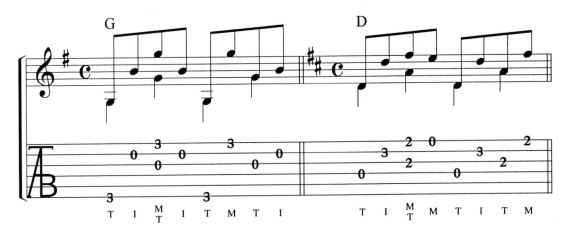

or:

In E:

Sus feel:

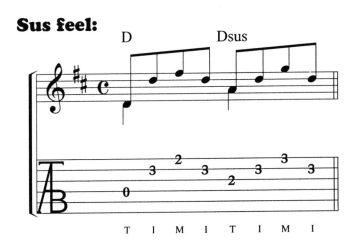

RHYTHM — BALLAD FEEL

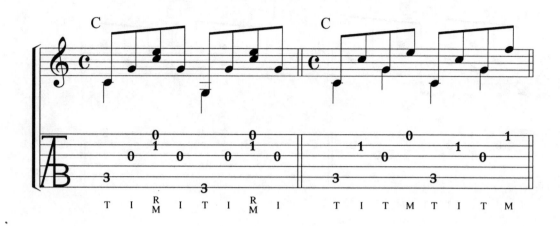

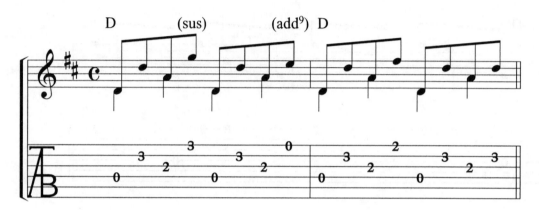

Pattern in C

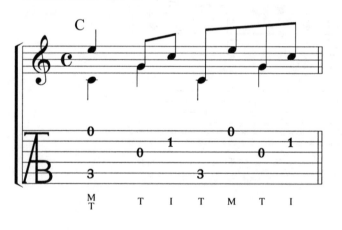

ii-vi-V-I in D

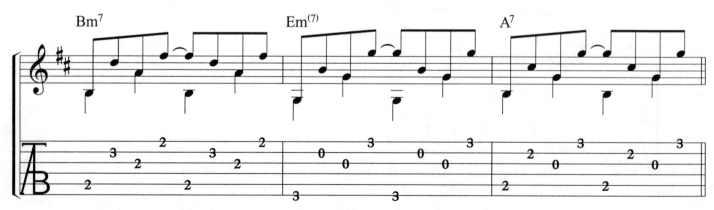

Major 7th Vamps

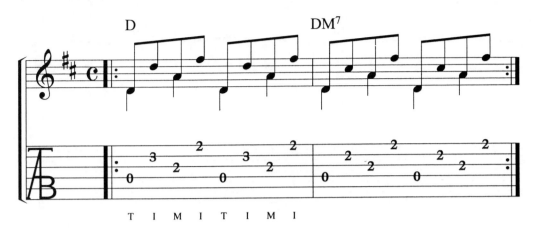

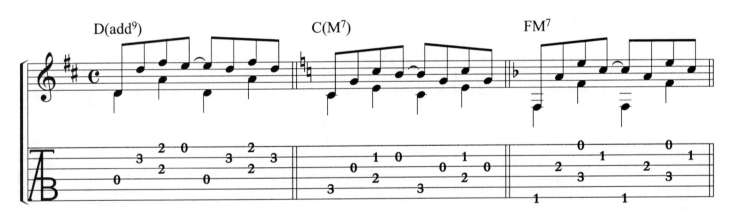

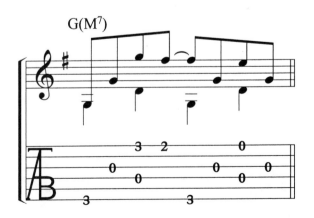

Progression in D

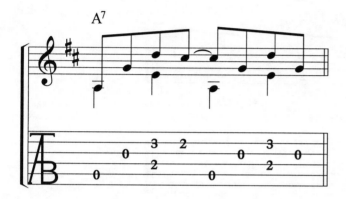

Progression in C

LEAD EXAMPLE — "JAZZED UP" RED RIVER VALLEY

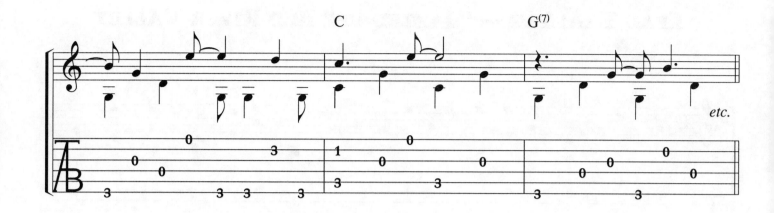

LEAD EXAMPLE — AURA LEE ON BASS STRINGS

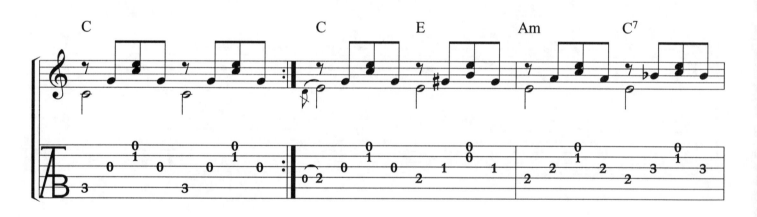

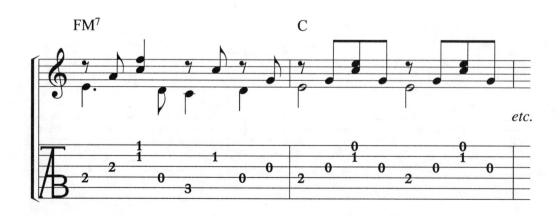

RHYTHM — HALF TIME FEEL

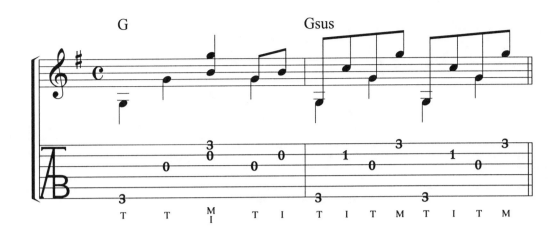

With vi-ii-V-I Progression/Key of C

RHYTHM — SHUFFLE BEAT

Key of E

Key of G

Melody Example

Shuffle Patterns in G

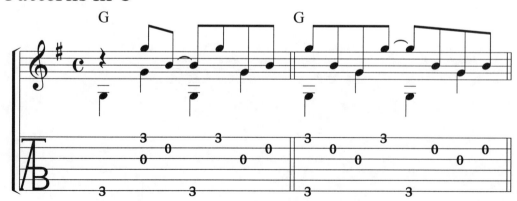

12

"Elvira feel"   **"Filled in":**

Up to D:

Up to E:

ASCENDING/DESCENDING BASS LINE PROGRESSIONS

Progression in G, simple chords

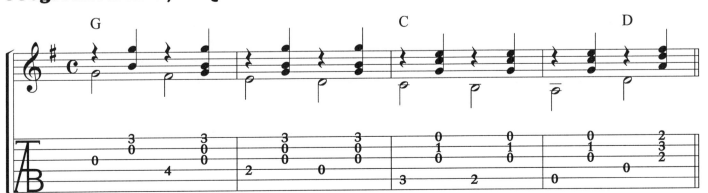

Progression in G, with substitute chords

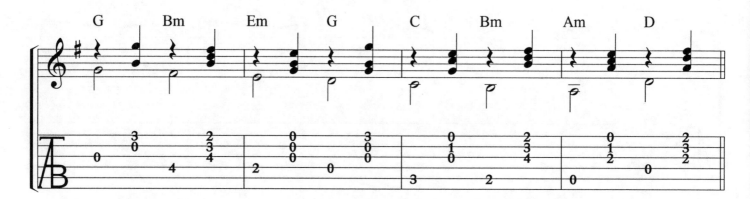

For progressions that go up and down the scale:

For this scale/note:	I	II	III	IV	V	VI	VII
use this chord type:	I	ii	iii	IV	V	ii	V
or this chord type:			I			I	IV	iii
or:							vi	

Note: lower case indicates minor chord, e.g. iii = IIIm

Ascending Bass Line in C

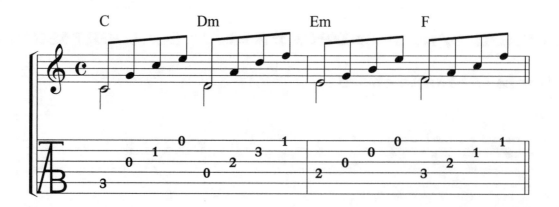

14

LESSON TWO
RAGTIME & RAGGY BLUES & JAZZ

STEALIN'

C   C⁷
Put your arms around me like a circle 'round the sun.

 F
I wanna love you baby like your easy rider done.

     C G⁷ C F   C G⁷ C
You don't believe I'm sinkin', look at the hole I'm in.

     C G⁷ C F   C G⁷ C
You don't believe I love you, look at the fool I've been.

  C   C⁷   F   Fm
Stealin', stealin', pretty Mama don'cha tell on me.

   C   G⁷   C C⁷ F Fm C G⁷
I'm stealin' back to my same old used to be.

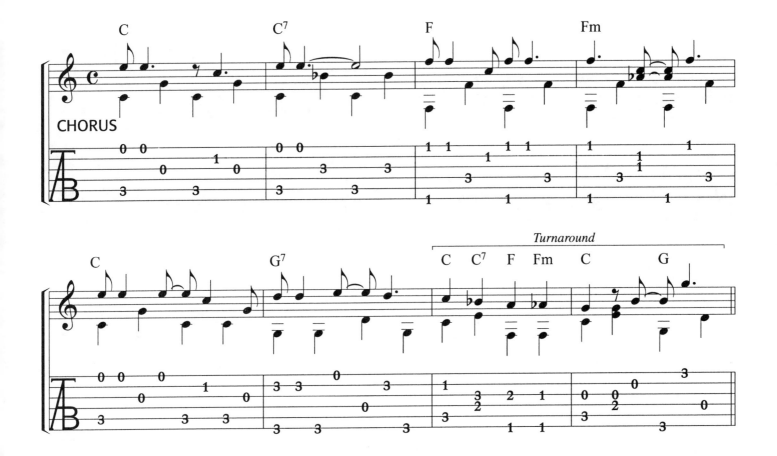

15

COCAINE

C   C^7 F
Walked down Tenth Street, turned up Main, Lookin' for the man who sells cocaine,

C G^7 C F C
Cocaine, run all 'round my brain.

E^7 F
Come here Mama, come here quick. This cocaine's makin' me sick.

C G^7 C C^7 F Fm C G^7
Cocaine, run all 'round my brain.

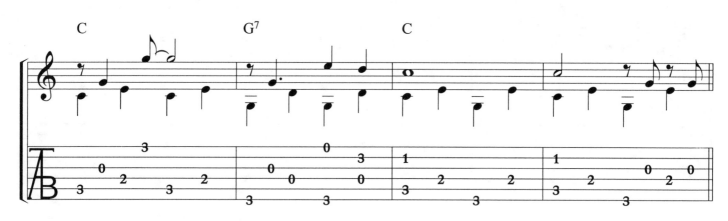

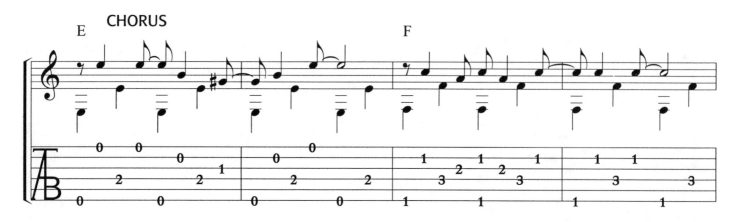

16

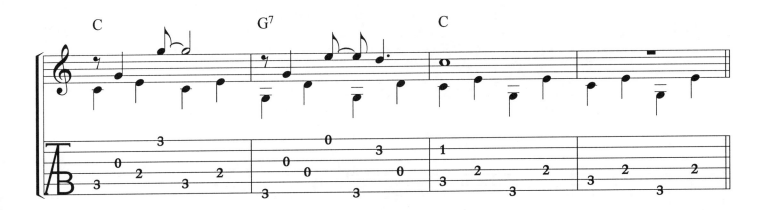

OH BABE, IT AIN'T NO LIE

<pre>
C   C⁷   F   C   F G⁷ C
One old woman in this town keeps tellin' her lies on me,
           C⁷   F   C   F G⁷ C
Wish to my soul that woman would die and stop tellin' those lies on me.
G⁷   C   E⁷   F
Oh babe, it ain't no lie, Oh babe, it ain't no lie,
                C   F   G⁷   C
Oh babe, it ain't no lie, You kow this life I'm livin' is mighty high.
</pre>

CHORUS

THE CIRCLE OF FIFTHS

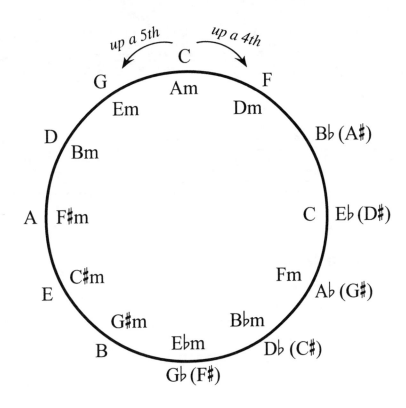

VI-II-V-I Progression in C

VI-II-V-I Progression in G

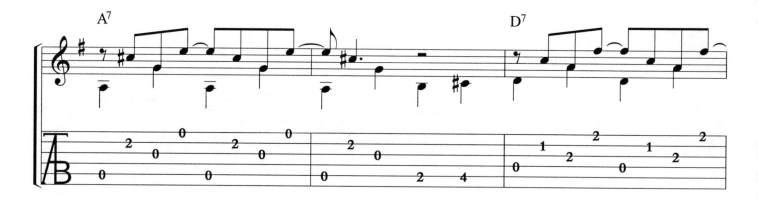

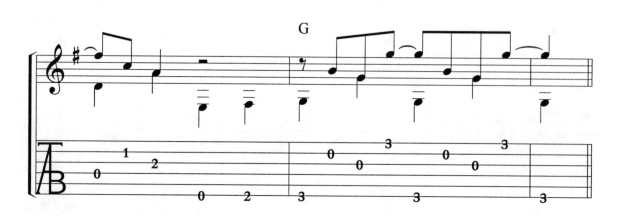

BILL BAILEY

C
Won't you come home Bill Bailey, won't you come home?

                                      G^7
She mourned the whole night long.

I'll do the cookin' honey, I'll pay the rent.

                        C
You know I done you wrong.

C
Remember that rainy evening I threw you out

  C^7 F
With nothing but a fine-tooth comb?

           Fm   C A^7
I know I'm to blame. Ain't that a shame?

  D^7 G^7 C
Bill Bailey, won't you please come home?

F (D form.)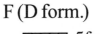

Fm (Dm form.)

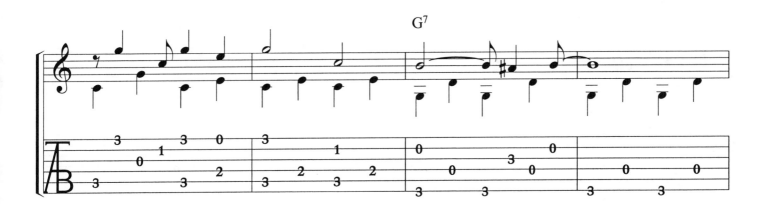

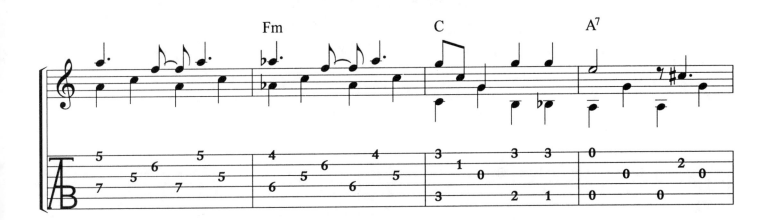

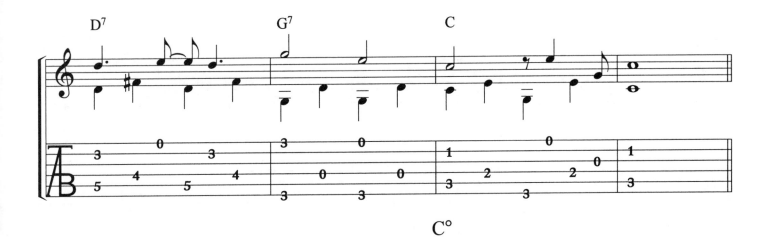

Diminished chord shape:

C°

Big Bill Broonzy

23

MAPLE LEAF RAG

THE ENTERTAINER

PART III

28

Brownie McGhee & Sticks McGhee

29

BULLY OF THE TOWN

30

CHORUS

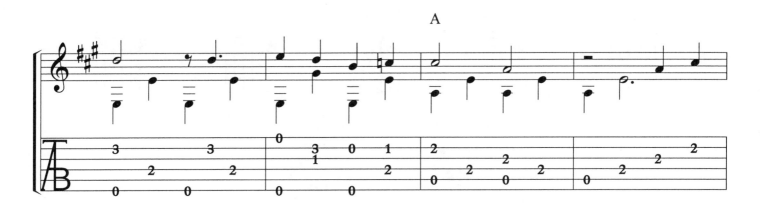

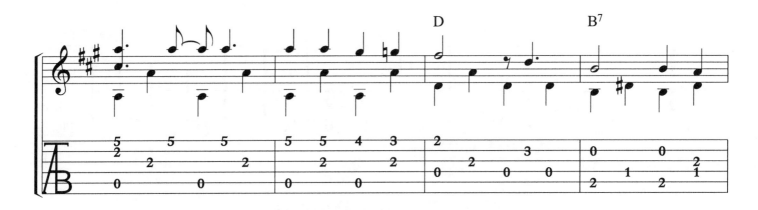

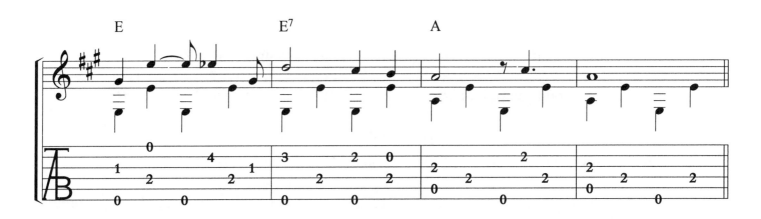

LESSON THREE
FINGERPICKING UP THE NECK

MOVEABLE CHORD FORMS
(Root is circled)

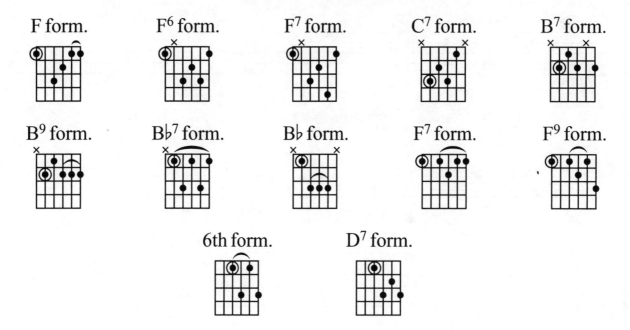

F form. F⁶ form. F⁷ form. C⁷ form. B⁷ form.

B⁹ form. B♭⁷ form. B♭ form. F⁷ form. F⁹ form.

6th form. D⁷ form.

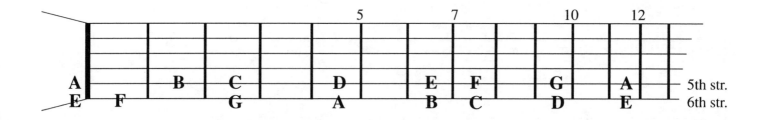

NINE POUND HAMMER

G   C⁷   G   D⁷   G
Nine pound hammer is a little too heavy, for my size, buddy, for my size.
                                               C⁷   G   D⁷   G
Roll on buddy, pull your load of coal. How can I pull when the wheels won't go?

I'm goin' on the mountain for to see my baby. Never coming back, never coming back.
Roll on buddy, pull your load of coal. How can I roll when the wheels won't go?

It's a long way to Harlan, and a long way to Hazard, To get a little brew, a little home brew.
Roll on buddy, don't you roll so slow. How can I pull when the wheels won't go?

Melody

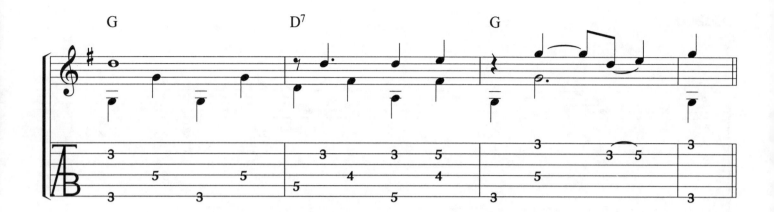

WABASH CANNONBALL

F Bb^7
Listen to the jingle, the rumble and the roar,

           C^7 F
As she glides along the woodlands, through hills and by the shore.

F Bb^7
Hear the mighty rush of engines, hear the lonesome hoboes call,

C^7 F
Travelin' through the jungles on the Wabash Cannonball.

Instrumental

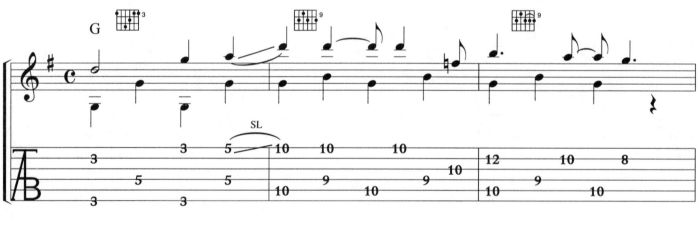

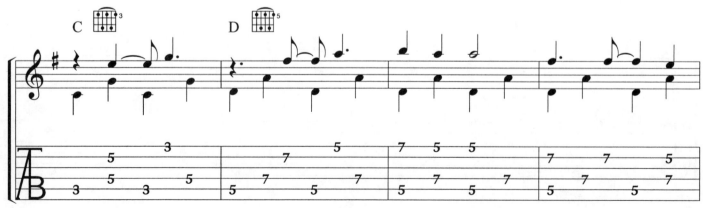

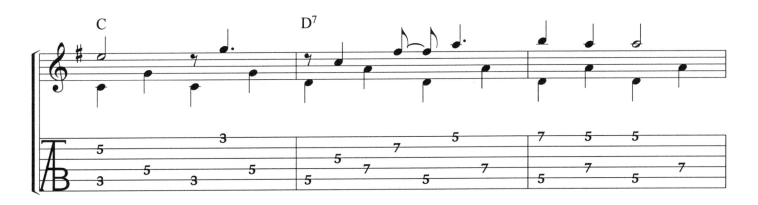

CAN THE CIRCLE BE UNBROKEN

F   B♭⁷   F

Can the circle be unbroken? Bye and bye, Lord, bye and bye.

F   C⁷   F

There's a better home a-waitin' in the sky, Lord, in the sky.

F Form accompaniment (in F)

Bb Form accompaniment (in F)

etc.

NINE POUND HAMMER

Accompaniment in C

CAN THE CIRCLE BE UNBROKEN

Melody (in F)

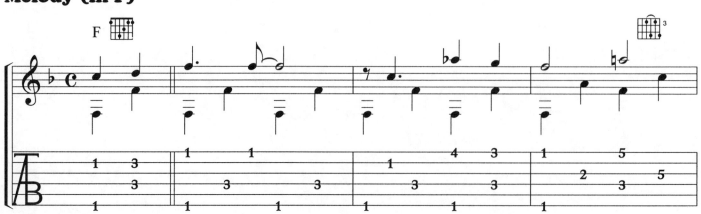

BURY ME BENEATH THE WILLOW

F   Bb   F   C⁷
My heart is sad and I'm so lonely, thinking of the one I love.

        F   Bb   F   C⁷   F
When will I see her? Oh no, never, unless we meet in heaven above.

        F   Bb   F   C⁷
Won't you bury me beneath the willow? Under the weeping willow tree.

F   Bb   F   C⁷   F
When she hears that I am sleeping, maybe then she'll think of me.

Melody

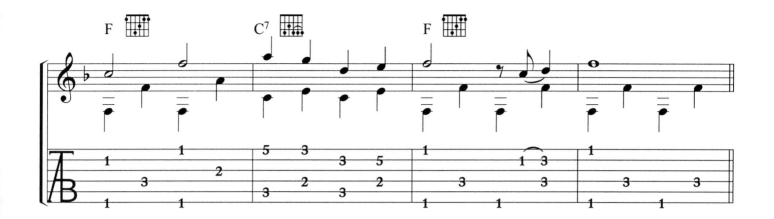

Rockabilly Break

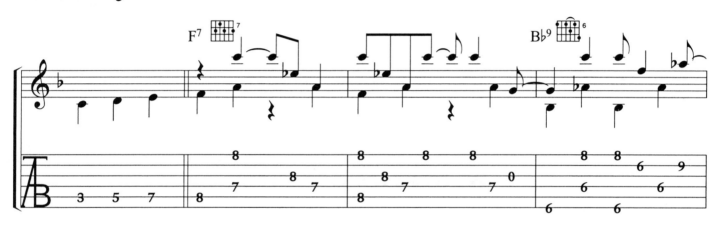

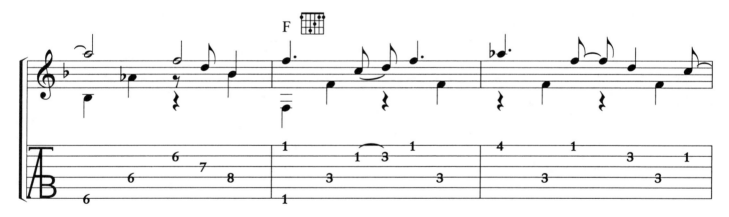

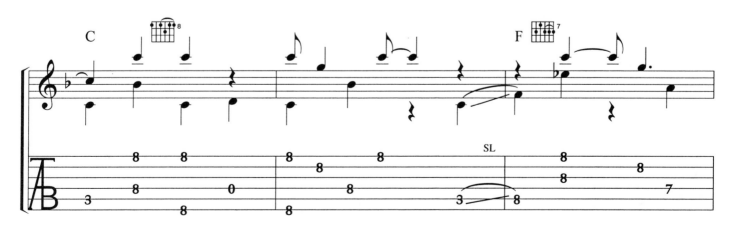

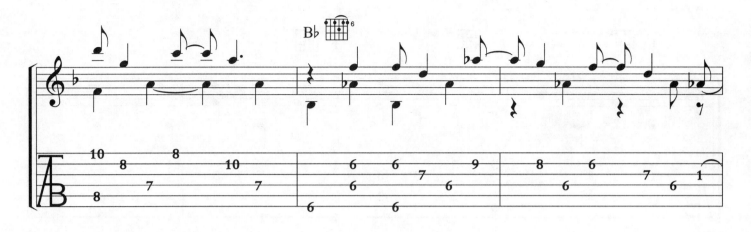

NINE POUND HAMMER

Rockabilly Break

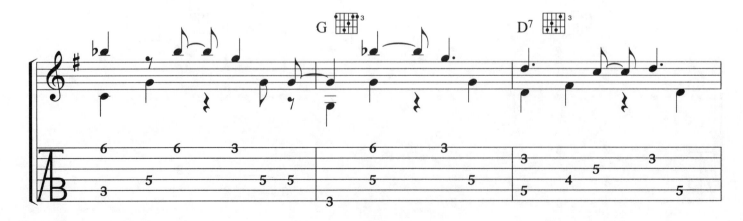

Two Chord Families

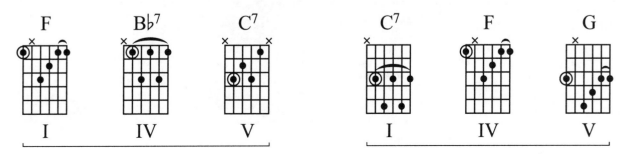

Fred Sokolow Video Guitar Lessons

We offer a wide variety of video lessons focusing on various aspects of fingerstyle guitar styles and techniques. These range from country blues to fingerstyle jazz, from the picking styles of Chet Atkins to the jazz motifs of Larry Coryell. Our teachers read like a "Who's Who" in the guitar world. They include: Chet Atkins, Martin Taylor, John Fahey, Pat Kirtley, Larry Coryell, John Renbourn, Stefan Grossman, Duck Baker, El McMeen, Marcel Dadi, Dave Van Ronk, Woody Mann, Pat Donohue, Fred Sokolow, Buster B. Jones, Ernie Hawkins, John Miller and others.

Our video lessons present the finest in clear and incisive visual education. Each tune is performed in full and then explained. This is usually followed by the piece played slowly on a split screen that allows the student to clearly see both the right and left hand movements. Everything played during the split screen segments is transcribed. All the video lessons include a free tab/music booklet.

We have indicated the duration, page length of the tab/music booklet and the grade level for each lesson.

All the videos in these pages can be order from Stefan Grossman's Guitar Workshop, PO Box 802, Sparta, NJ 07871 or via our website at www.guitar.videos.com.

Code for our Level Gradations:

Level 1: For the beginner. You know the basics of your instrument. These lessons will help establish a strong playing foundation.

Level 2: For the advanced beginner/early intermediate. You have been playing awhile and feel comfortable with your instrument. These lessons will help develop your repertoire and expand your techniques and explore new styles.

Level 3: For the intermediate student. You play well and are looking for challenges and new directions.

Level 4: For the advanced player. You are ready to tackle anything!

The Music Of Paul Simon
Arranged for Fingerstyle Guitar
Taught by Fred Sokolow
* *

90-min video • Level 2
80 page tab/music booklet
GW 501 $29.95
* *

featuring The Boxer, Scarborough Fair, American Tune, Bridge Over Troubled Water, Mrs. Robinson, Hearts and Bones, Me and Julio Down By The Schoolyard, 59th Street Bridge Song (Feelin' Groovy) and Mother and Child Reunion

The Music Of Bob Dylan
Arranged for Fingerstyle Guitar
Taught by Fred Sokolow
* *

90-min video • Level 2
72 page tab/music booklet
GW 502 $29.95
* *

featuring Lay Lady Lay, My Back Pages, I Shall Be Released, Blowin' In The Wind, Don't Think Twice, Mr. Tambourine Man, Just Like Tom Thumb's Blues, Too Much Of Nothing and The Times They Are A Changing

The Music of the Grateful Dead
Arranged for Fingerstyle Guitar
Taught by Fred Sokolow
* *

92-min video • Level 2
80 page tab/music booklet
GW 503 $29.95
* *

featuring Friend of the Devil, Ripple, Sugar Magnolia, Touch Of Grey, Uncle John's Band, Truckin', Alabama Getaway, Dire Wolf and Deal

Learn how to play and sing classic Paul Simon, Bob Dylan and Grateful Dead tunes from start to finish. Each of these video lessons will teach you how to fingerpick backup arrangements while singing, how to play instrumental solos and how to begin and end each song. While studying Fred Sokolow's arrangements you will also learn a lot about fingerpicking: backup patterns, soloing ideas and various chord positions.

Each song is played at regular speed and then slowed down with a split-screen that gives you a close-up look at the picking as well as chording hand. All the arrangements are clearly written out in tab and music in the accompanying booklet along with lead sheets and lyrics.

Beginner's Blues Guitar
Taught by Fred Sokolow
* *
70-min video • Level 1
48 page tab/music booklet
GW 401 $29.95
* *

In this video lesson, Fred Sokolow starts at the very beginning: tuning up and playing simple chords but by the end of this lesson you will be playing the blues in several keys, strumming and fingerpicking. You'll learn how to play:
• *Blues turnarounds.*
• *Boogie Woogie bass lines.*
• *Several strumming and fingerpicking patterns.*
• *Blues solos, licks and accompaniment styles of Lightnin' Hopkins, Big Bill Broonzy, Jimmy Reed and Mississippi John Hurt.*
• *Classic blues tunes like How Long Blues, Keys To The Highway, Baby What You Want Me To Do, Blues With a Feeling and Hesitation Blues.*

Bottleneck Slide Guitar
Acoustic & Electric Guitar Techniques
Taught by Fred Sokolow
* *
73-min video • Level 1/2
56 page tab/music booklet
GW 409 $29.95
* *

Nothing sounds as bluesy as a slide guitar, and this 70 minute video shows you how it's done on electric and acoustic, solo or with a group. Using classic blues tunes – *Little Red Rooster, Sittin' On Top Of The World, Reconsider Baby, The Sky Is Crying, Farther On Up The Road* and *One Way Out* – Fred Sokolow shows you how to play and improvise slide in the styles of the great bluesmen – Muddy Waters, Elmore James, Mississippi Fred McDowell and Duane Allman.
In this video lesson you will learn:
• *Solos, backup licks, turnarounds and fills in three tunings: open G, open D and standard.*
• *How to play slide in any key.*
• *How to improvise solos in standard and open tunings using moveable blues boxes.*

Electric Blues Guitar
Taught by Fred Sokolow
* *
80-min video • Level 2
48 page tab/music booklet
GW 404 $29.95
* *

If you want to play blues guitar like B.B. King, Eric Clapton or Buddy Guy then this 80 minute video will get you on track. You'll learn:
• *Moveable scale patterns and licks.*
• *Moveable chords and chord based licks.*
• *How to play melodies, chord backup and improvised solos on blues classics Stormy Monday, Everyday I Have The Blues, Killing Floor and Baby Please Don't Go.*
• *Intros and endings.*
• *Enough theory to understand the 12-bar blues structure and be able to play backup and solo in any key.*
• *Boogie bass lines, vibrato, note-bending and more.*

Beginner's Fingerpicking Guitar
Taught by Fred Sokolow
* *
70-min video • Level 1
48 page tab/music booklet
GW 402 $29.95
* *

Fingerpicking is essential to the blues, country, rock and folk music and it's a way to solo or accompany your own singing. By the end of this session you will know how to play:
• *Several fingerpicking patterns/rhythm grooves*
• *Chords and licks in five different keys.*
• *Connecting "bass runs" in all five keys.*
• *Lots of well known tunes including Stealin', Stagolee, Wabash Cannonball, Nine Pound Hammer, Sloop John B, Jamaica Farewell, St. James Infirmary, Careless Love, House Of The Rising Sun and Scarborough Fair.*
• *Melodies and alternating bass at the same time.*

Fingerpicking Guitar Solos
Taught by Fred Sokolow
* *
55-min video • Level 1/2
40 page tab/music booklet
GW 408 $29.95
* *

This video is the follow-up lesson to Fred Sokolow's *BEGINNER'S FINGERPICKING GUITAR.* It presents six classic fingerpicking tunes – solos and accompaniments – with a bluesy and country flavor: *Creole Belle, Hesitation Blues, Sitting On Top Of The World, Ain't Nobody's Business, Hey Hey Hey* and *Blues For Dixie.* Fred plays and sings each arrangement up to speed and then slows them down explaining any unusual or difficult licks. Along the way you will also be taught:
• *How to fingerpick in several keys*
• *Soloing and accompaniment in standard, dropped D and open D tunings*
• *Moveable chord formations*
• *Several major scales*
• *A fingerpicking scale exercise*

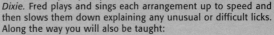

Rockabilly Guitar
Taught by Fred Sokolow
* *
73-min video • Level 2
48 page tab/music booklet
GW 403 $29.95
* *

Rockabilly is the roots of rock. It combines electric blues, country blues, Merle Travis-style fingerpicking and more. Using classic rockabilly tunes like *Blue Suede Shoes, Little Sister, That's All Right Mama, Matchbox Blues* and *That'll Be The Day,* Fred Sokolow shows the styles and techniques needed to play rockabilly guitar solos and backup. By the end of this hour-plus session, you'll know how to play:
• *Boogie Woogie backup licks and Turnarounds.*
• *Classic key of E blues/rock licks.*
• *Moveable blues/rock scales*
• *Fingerpicking patterns.*
• *Licks and solos of Buddy Holly, Carl Perkins, Eddie Cochran, Scotty Moore and Chuck Berry.*

Beginner's
Country Guitar
Taught by Fred Sokolow
* *
65-min video • Level 1/2
40 page tab/music booklet
GW 407 $29.95
* *

Country music is more popular than ever and all you need to put over a good country song is your voice and a guitar. This video gives you the tools you need to play old-fashioned country, honky-tonk and country rock. Playing classics like *Blue Eyes Crying In The Rain, I'm So Lonesome I Could Cry, The Bottle Let Me Down, I'm Movin' On, Will The Circle Be Unbroken, Silver Wings* and *Jambalaya,* Fred Sokolow shows you the basics of country guitar. You'll learn how to play: *Accompaniment strums for different rhythmic feels • A variety of first-position chords • Bass runs • Major scales • Solos and turnarounds*

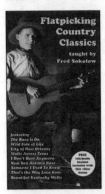

Flatpicking
Country Classics
Taught by Fred Sokolow
* *
92-min video • Level 1/2
64 page tab/music booklet
GW 410 $29.95
* *

All you need to put over a good country song is your voice and a guitar. In this video Fred teaches nine standards every country picker/singer should know. You'll learn an intro for each song, a backup pattern and bass runs to play while singing, an instrumental solo, and an ending.

Picking up where his **BEGINNER'S COUNTRY GUITAR** video left off, Fred keeps the arrangements fairly simple but includes a few up-the-neck chord positions and hot licks. You'll learn solos and runs in five different keys. Each song is played at regular speed and then slowed down on a split-screen that gives you a close-up look at the picking hand and the chording hand. All the arrangements are clearly written out in tab and music in the accompanying booklet, along with lyrics.

Titles include: New San Antonio Rose, Wild Side of Life, Waltz Across Texas, The Race is On, Beautiful Kentucky Waltz, That's the Way Love Goes, I Don't Hurt Any more, Someone I Used To Know and City of New Orleans

Jazz Chord Solos
for Beginners
Taught by Fred Sokolow
* *
84-min video • Level 2
48 page tab/music booklet
GW 411 $29.95
* *

In this video, you'll learn six timeless tunes from start to finish: how to play backup while you sing them, and how to play a beautiful chord-melody solo/instrumental for each song. The tunes are arranged for beginners: there are no difficult chords, and Fred goes over the tricky spots in each tune before playing it...then you'll watch him replay the song, slower, on a split screen with close-ups of both hands. Just for fun, Fred includes the rarely-heard introductory verses to three of the songs. Best of all, you can read all six arrangements (tablature, music and chord grids) in the booklet that comes with this video. Chord soloing (playing the melody and chords at the same time) is a very complete and satisfying guitar style. This lesson will get you started and Fred's relaxed teaching style makes it easy.

Titles include: Summertime, Fly Me To the Moon, Georgia On My Mind, It Had To Be You, What a Wonderful World and Ain't Misbehavin'.

Playing &
Understanding
Jazz Guitar
Taught by Fred Sokolow
* *
75-min video Level 2/3
40 page tab/music booklet
GW 406 $29.95
* *

Jazz is one of the most challenging and satisfying styles of music you can play on the guitar. This video lesson presents a very clear and thorough introduction to jazz guitar. You will study all the licks, chords, scales and theory that you will need to know to get started. In this 75 minute lesson Fred Sokolow shows you:

- Chord construction and chord types, including inversions and diminished chords.
- Scalewise progressions and how to use them.
- Circle-of-fifths progressions and how to play and recognize them.
- Chord comping, chord soloing and playing single-note solos to standards like *I Got Rhythm, Honeysuckle Rose* and *Watch What Happens.*
- How to improvise solos using scales and chord-based licks.
- How to solo over II-V-I standard changes.

Beginner's
Rock Guitar
Taught by Fred Sokolow
* *
72-min video • Level 1/2
64 page tab/music booklet
GW 405 $29.95
* *

Before rock' n' roll became a big corporate industry, playing rock guitar used to be the most fun you could have with your pants on! Fred Sokolow shows why in this video that uses your favorite garage-band tunes to demonstrate how to:

- Play power-chord backup in any key – the Louie Louie way.
- Solo and play Chuck Berry style boogie backup on tunes like Roll Over Beethoven and School Days
- Use blues scales and "substitute" scales for soloing.
- Solo with sliding major pentatonic scales in the styles of Dickey Betts and Jerry Garcia.
- Play tunes and more tunes: Stand By Me, Midnight Hour, My Girl, The Wind Cries Mary, Let It Be, Proud Mary and others.

Fred Sokolow Book/CD Audio Lessons

Learn how to play and sing classic Paul Simon, Bob Dylan and Grateful Dead tunes from start to finish. Each of these book/CD lessons will teach you how to fingerpick backup arrangements while singing, how to play instrumental solos and how to begin and end each song. While studying Fred Sokolow's arrangements you will also learn a lot about fingerpicking: backup patterns, soloing ideas and various chord positions.

Each song is played at regular speed and then slowed down. All the arrangements are clearly written out in tab and music in the accompanying book along with lead sheets and lyrics. Each book comes with two CDs that feature the audio tracks from the video lessons of the same titles. Please note that the Paul Simon and Bob Dylan packages each feature two CDs and the booklet is sized at 5x7 and is packaged in the CD case. All our other book/CD titles have books sized 9x12 and the CDs as fixed to the front and back book covers.

The Music of
Paul Simon
Taught by
Fred Sokolow
featuring The Boxer, Bridge Over Troubled Water, Scarborough Fair, American Tune, Mrs. Robinson, Hearts and Bones, Me and Julio Down By The Schoolyard, 59th Street Bridge Song (Feelin' Groovy) & Mother and Child Reunion

64 page tab/music booklet (dimension 5x7) with two compact discs. GW97814 $14.95

The Music of
Bob Dylan
Taught by
Fred Sokolow
featuring Lay Lady Lay, My Back Pages, I Shall Be Released, Blowin' In The Wind, Don't Think Twice, Mr. Tambourine Man, Just Like Tom Thumb's Blues, Too Much Of Nothing & The Times They Are A Changing

56 page tab/music booklet (dimension 5x7) with two compact discs. GW97815 $14.95

The Music of
The Grateful Dead
Taught by
Fred Sokolow
featuring Friend of the Devil, Ripple, Sugar Magnolia, Touch Of Grey, Uncle John's Band, Truckin', Alabama Getaway, Dire Wolf & Deal

56 page tab/music book with two compact discs. GW99408 $24.95

Beginner's Blues Guitar
Taught by
Fred Sokolow

Starting from ground zero, Fred teaches you to play blues guitar. For the beginner guitarist. 48 page tab/music book with three compact discs.

LESSON ONE: SIMPLE BLUES IN E: Strum blues in the style of Lightnin' Hopkins, Big Bill Broonzy and John Lee Hooker. Simple chords and accompaniment, boogie bass lines and turnarounds.

LESSON TWO: SIMPLE BLUES IN G AND C: The ideas of the first lesson are expanded. Techniques of Mance Lipscomb, Mississippi John Hurt and Blind Blake are presented.

LESSON THREE: PLAYING MELODY: Simple first position blues scales needed for soloing (both fingerpicking and flatpicking) in the keys of E, G and C. Discussion of lead breaks and choking strings. *GW98506 $24.95*

Bottleneck/Slide Guitar
Taught by
Fred Sokolow

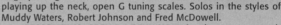

This series of lessons is designed to start you playing and improvising with slide guitar (either acoustic or electric). For the beginner to intermediate student. 40 page tab/music book with three compact discs.

LESSON ONE: OPEN G TUNING: Simple chords, playing down the neck, fingerpicking hints, barred chords, playing up the neck, open g tuning scales. Solos in the styles of Muddy Waters, Robert Johnson and Fred McDowell.

LESSON TWO: OPEN D & E TUNING: Using the same approach as Lesson One, the concentration is now focused on Open D and Open E tunings. Solos in the style of Tampa Red, Elmore James and Duane Allman.

LESSON THREE: STANDARD TUNING: Playing in the styles of Robert Nighthawk, George Harrison and Ron Wood. Scales and positions. *GW98513 $24.95*

Rockabilly Guitar
Taught by
Fred Sokolow

For the intermediate guitarist. 40 page tab/music book with three compact discs.

LESSON ONE: FIRST POSITION LICKS - Key of E and key of A rural blues licks are the foundation of rockabilly guitar. Twelve-bar blues progressions and chord families, boogie bass lines and backup figures, turnaround licks and patterns.

LESSON TWO: PLAYING UP THE NECK - Chords and chord families that allow you to play all the lead and backup licks from Lesson One up the neck in any key are discussed. Fingerpicking melodies up the neck, easy chord-fragment-based licks, moveable boogie bass backup and moveable rockabilly riffs and cliches are featured.

LESSON THREE: PUTTING IT ALL TOGETHER ROCKABILLY STYLE - Moveable blues/rock scales (single and double-note) used in rockabilly music are taught. *GW98512 $24.95*

CD Track Listings

The audio lessons in this series were originally recorded in the 1970s. They were initially released on audio cassettes. We have gone back to our master tapes to get the best possible sound for this new CD edition. The complete contents of the original recordings have been maintained but certain references to albums that are no longer available or information that is out of date have been edited out .

These lessons originally came with different print material. These were handwritten and in some cases offered only tab transcriptions. The lessons have now been typeset in tab/music. As a result some spoken references on the CDs regarding page numbers or a position of a line or phrase on a page may differ slightly from the written tab/music in this new edition. We have annotated as carefully and exactly as possible what each track on the CDs present. Please use these track descriptions as your reference guide.

Lesson One

Track 1: Introduction
Track 2: Tuning
Track 3: Teaching of chords commonly used in pop songs
Track 4: Teaching of commonly used chord progressions
Track 5: Teaching of commonly used rhythm patterns
Track 6: Teaching of variations of picking patterns
Track 7: Teaching of picking pattern for rock ballads
Track 8: Teaching of picking patterns for accompanying a vocal
Track 9: Teaching of variations for ballad picking
Track 10: Teaching playing leads with thumb beat

Track 11: Fred plays *Red River Valley*
Track 12: Teaching of *Red River Valley*
Track 13: Teaching of rock ballad in halftime
Track 14: Teaching of picking over a shuffle beat/boogie woogie
Track 15: Teaching of playing melody over a shuffle beat
Track 16: Teaching of variations of fingerpicking slow shuffle beats
Track 17: Teaching of speeding up the pattern
Track 18: Teaching of moving bass lines in pop music
Track 19: Teaching of variations of moving bass lines
Track 20: Closing thoughts

Lesson Two

Track 1: Introduction
Track 2: Tuning
Track 3: Discussion of turnarounds
Track 4: Fred plays *Stealin'*
Track 5: Teaching of *Stealin'*
Track 6: Fred plays *Cocaine*
Track 7: Teaching of *Cocaine*
Track 8: Fred plays *Oh Babe, Ain't No Lie*
Track 9: Teaching of *Oh Babe, Ain't No Lie*
Track 10: Teaching of Circle of Fifths
Track 11: Fred plays examples of ragtime progressions
Track 12: Fred continues playing examples of ragtime progressions
Track 13: Fred plays *Bill Bailey*
Track 14: Teaching of *Bill Bailey*
Track 15: Fred plays slowly *Bill Bailey* using various ragtime techniques

Track 16: Teaching of Circle of Fifths exercise
Track 17: Discussion of ragtime fingerpicking
Track 18: Fred plays *Maple Leaf Rag*
Track 19: Teaching of *Maple Leaf Rag*
Track 20: Fred plays *The Entertainer*
Track 21: Teaching of *The Entertainer*
Track 22: Fred plays *Bully Of The Town*
Track 23: Fred plays slowly *Bully Of The Town*
Track 24: Teaching of verse of *Bully Of The Town*
Track 25: Teaching of chorus of *Bully Of The Town*
Track 26: Fred plays Circle of Fifths in the key of C
Track 27: Fred plays Circle of Fifths in the key of G
Track 28: Fred plays Circle of Fifths in the key of D
Track 29: Fred plays Circle of Fifths in the key of A

Lesson Three

Track 1: Introduction
Track 2: Tuning
Track 3: Teaching of moveable chords
Track 4: Teaching of more moveable formations
Track 5: Teaching of third variation with fifth string as root
Track 6: Fred plays *Nine Pound Hammer*
Track 7: Teaching of *Nine Pound Hammer*
Track 8: Fred plays *Nine Pound Hammer* and continues teaching
Track 9: Fred plays *Nine Pound Hammer* with melody
Track 10: Teaching of *Nine Pound Hammer* with melody
Track 11: Fred plays slowly *Nine Pound Hammer* with melody
Track 12: A review of changing keys with moveable chords
Track 13: Discussion of picking techniques
Track 14: Fred plays *Wabash Cannonball*
Track 15: Teaching of *Wabash Cannonball*
Track 16: Fred plays slowly *Wabash Cannonball*
Track 17: Continuation of teaching of *Wabash Cannonball*
Track 18: Fred introduces *Will The Circle Be Unbroken*

Track 19: Fred play *Will The Circle Be Unbroken*
Track 20: Teaching of *Will The Circle Be Unbroken*
Track 21: Fred play *Will The Circle Be Unbroken*
Track 22: Teaching of a new variation of F fingering making it a seventh chord
Track 23: Discussion of another chord family
Track 24: Fred plays *Wabash Cannonball* starting with A/5th string root chord
Track 25: Teaching of new chords: A/4th string root chord
Track 26: Fred plays *Will The Circle Be Unbroken* and teaches the melody
Track 27: Fred plays slowly *Will The Circle Be Unbroken*
Track 28: Fred plays *Bury Me Beneath The Willow Tree*
Track 29: teaching of structure of *Bury Me Beneath The Willow Tree*
Track 30: Teaching of melody of *Bury Me Beneath The Willow Tree*
Track 31: Discussion of rockabilly playing
Track 32: Teaching of rockabilly lead break
Track 33: Fred plays a rockabilly lead break for *Nine Pound Hammer*
Track 34: Closing thoughts